Open Hands,
Open Heart,
The Story of
Biddy Mason

To: Oretheal T. Halthon —
You are a lovely lady. Please
continue to live with open
hands and a loving heart.

Deidre Robinson
2-8-99

OPEN HANDS, OPEN HEART
The Story of
BIDDY MASON

Deidre Robinson
Illustrations by **Albert T. Cooper III**

Introduction by
Reverend Cecil L. "Chip" Murray
and
Supervisor Yvonne Braithwaite Burke

SLY FOX PUBLISHING COMPANY
Gardena, California

Acknowledgements

My sincere thanks to Dean Brown, Rev. Cecil Murray, Yvonne Braithwaite Burke,
Al and Adoria Cooper, Aloria Character, Karen Slade,
Ken Bentley, Erithe Smith, Tony Forge, Terry Dunnahoo and Arvid Knudsen
for their encouragement and contribution to this book.

Published by Sly Fox Publishing Company

Designed and produced by Arvid Knudsen
Electronic composition and production by DAK Graphics

Library of Congress Cataloging-in-Publication Data
Deidre Robinson
Open Hands, open heart: the story of Biddy Mason / Deidre Robinson
illustrations by Albert T. Cooper III; introductions by
Cecil L. "Chip" Murray and Yvonne Braithwaite Burke – 1st edition
p. cm
Includes index
Preassigned LCCN: 97-91110
ISBN 0-9660618-0-2
Summary: After her master moves his household to California, a slave
midwife successfully sues for her freedom and goes on to found an
Afro-American church and fourteen area nursing homes.

1. Mason, Biddy, 1818-1891 – Juvenile literature. 2. Slaves-
United States -- Biography -- Juvenile literature. 3. Los Angeles (Calif.) –
Biography -- Juvenile literature. 4. Afro-American midwives –
Juvenile literature. I. Cooper, Albert T., III. Title.

E444.M37R63 1998   305.5'67'092 [B]
                                QB197-41255

Printed and Bound in Singapore

1 2 3 4 5   02 01 00 99 98

I dedicate this book
to my mother,
Mary B. Robinson,
who also has
open hands and an open heart.
To my family, friends and students,
I am thankful
for your love and support.

From Albert: To my parents,
Al and Adoria Cooper

INTRO[D]

by Rev. Cecil L. "Chip" Murray,
*Senior Minister, First African
Methodist Episcopal Church*

B IDDY MASON is chronicled in the hearts of those who are heirs to her legacy – people who are struggling against the odds of all forms of slavery, denial, impoverishment, and seeming hopelessness. Here is a slave woman who determines with her God not only to escape Pharaoh, but to dwell in a new land in prosperity, and to erect a monument to the God of liberation who made her dreams a reality. A part of that monument is the edifice that stands today as the oldest black congregation in Los Angeles, some 14,000 sons and daughters of Biddy, dedicated to the same ideals that made Mama Mason a lighthouse pointing the way to possibilities. The author, like the one who inspires her writing, has done superbly well.

CTION

by Yvonne Braithwaite Burke
Supervisor, Second District
Board of Supervisors County of Los Angeles

B IDDY MASON is one of my true heroines. The
amazing achievements and courage of Biddy
Mason provide a new perspective to the history of
California in the era of slavery. The life of Biddy Mason
can provide inspiration to young people of color who
find themselves overwhelmed by the pressures and bur-
den of existence in the inner city or poverty.

Every woman or man, young or old, who thinks
they are faced with seemingly insurmountable barriers
can take heart and inspiration from the life and courage
of Biddy Mason.

No child who reads this story will ever forget this
legendary woman who struggled in the true frontier and
not only survived but flourished.

Picking cotton was brutal work.

The rays of the hot sun pounded on Biddy's back. Sweat oozed from every pore of her body making her clothes wet and heavy. Picking cotton was brutal. Her back and knees ached from the constant up and down motion. This work was even harder than usual because she was expecting her third child soon. Biddy tried not to prick her fingers on the twigs but it was nearly impossible not to do. Every night she rubbed an herbal medicine on her fingers to help them heal.

Biddy had a lot on her mind today. She was worried about her future. Rumors swirled around the slave quarters. The word heard from the big house was that Master Smith planned to move his family to Utah. Master Smith was a devout Mormon who wanted to live with others who shared his faith. He also planned to take some of his slaves with him, but no one knew which ones.

This rumor worried Biddy tremendously; the master had total power to separate entire families and Biddy did not want to lose her two little girls. That night, when Master Smith made his rounds through the slave quarters, he told Biddy that he planned to take her and all her children with him. Biddy was the strongest woman slave he owned and he needed her to herd his sheep. They would not leave until her baby was born. He also planned to take her sister Hannah and Hannah's children.

Biddy was angry and frustrated. She did not want to move, especially so soon after having

Master Smith planned to move to Utah.

Biddy worried that the master might sell her children.

her baby. But what choice did she have? She could not refuse to go. Master Smith would whip her severely for being disobedient. Even worse, he might sell her children. She was powerless and had to do what she was told. She was a slave and this was one of the many indignities she had to endure.

Biddy was born into slavery in Hancock County, Georgia, in 1818. She was given the name of Bridget, but throughout her life people called her by her nickname, "Biddy." Like most slaves, she was forbidden to learn how to read and write. Fortunately, she learned other skills which would prove valuable to her as an adult. How to tend to livestock, how to use herbs and roots to make medicine, nursing skills, and especially how to deliver babies.

When Biddy was 18 years old, she and her sister Hannah were sold to Robert Marion Smith in Logtown, Mississippi. Robert and his wife, Rebecca Crosby Smith, had six children. Biddy delivered all of the Smith children. Rebecca was very sickly and weak so Biddy had to care for her as well as her children.

After the first of the year, Biddy gave birth to her third daughter, Harriet. The Smith household left for Utah shortly afterwards. Utah was safe territory for Mormons to practice their faith. Mormons in the south and midwest had been attacked because people did not approve of their religious beliefs. After the murder of their first leader, Joseph Smith, their new leader, Brigham Young, chose Utah for a Mormon settlement.

Their journey began on March 10, 1848. They joined an expedition of 300 wagons led by John Brown, a Mormon guide. The journey was

Biddy learned her nursing skills and how to deliver babies
from the older slave midwives.

very difficult. They traveled thousands of miles through days of sweltering heat and freezing nights. Biddy, Hannah, and the other slaves rose well before daybreak to load the supplies onto the wagons, fix breakfast for Master Smith and his family, then dress and feed their children.

THE SMITH JOURNEY

An inventory of the Smith journey in 1848 included:
56 whites, 34 slaves, 7 milk cows,
2 yoke of oxen, 8 mules,
and dozens of covered wagons.

The covered wagons were filled with the supplies and belongings of the travelers, so the women and children took turns riding. Biddy and the rest of the slaves were never given a turn to ride. Biddy walked those thousands of miles through the prairie and the desert behind her owner's wagon. She carried her infant daughter

Biddy walked behind the wagons for thousands of miles.

in her arms. Her nine year old daughter Ellen and her four year old daughter Ann walked beside her.

Biddy was responsible for the sheep; they could not wander away from the wagon train. If any did stray, she found and led them back to the herd. Master Smith probably would have beaten Biddy if she had lost any of his sheep.

Biddy cared for her girls and tended to anyone who got sick. She also delivered babies. At night, an exhausted Biddy rubbed the soles of her feet, which had been severely cut by the blades of grass and sharp rocks, with an herbal oil from the plants she carried in her knapsack.

The Smith household arrived in Salt Lake City in November 1848. They lived in Utah for three years. When the Mormon church leaders decided to establish a new post in San Bernadino, California, Robert Smith moved his family again. In 1851, the Smith party journeyed with 150 wagons of Mormon pioneers.

Biddy would travel once more with the
family to California.

CALIFORNIA LAW

California's law against slavery did not prevent slaveholders from bringing their slaves into the state. Some owners did not know that California was a free state. The rest of the slaveowners were aware of the law but chose to ignore it.

Once again, Biddy endured another difficult journey. She walked behind her master's wagon and tended to the livestock, the sick, the Smiths as well as her own three girls.

Living in San Bernadino were Mormons and free blacks who had settled in the area after California was admitted to the Union in 1850. Biddy made friends with many people. It was from them that she learned slavery was against the law in California. Biddy, her daughters, and the rest of Smith's slaves were free!

Master Smith did not care that California was a free state. As far as he was concerned, his slaves were his property and he was keeping

Biddy learned that slavery was against
the law in California.

them. Many people believed Master Smith did not want to lose Biddy and Hannah because he had fathered their children.

The only way Master Smith could keep his slaves was to leave California. In 1855, he decided to move his household to Texas, which was a slave state. He had to wait to take the journey because Hannah was unable to travel. She was expecting another child shortly. Master Smith moved his entire household to the Santa Monica Mountains. He figured he could hide until it was safe to travel to Texas.

Naturally Biddy did not want to leave California. This was probably the only chance she and her three daughters had for freedom. Desperate for a solution, she confided in Charles Owens and Manuel Pepper, two young men who were friends of her daughter Ellen and one of her nieces. Charles and Manuel promised Biddy they would find a way to stop Smith.

Charles told his father, Robert Owens, about

Biddy did not want to leave California,
where she had a chance for freedom.

The sheriff found Biddy and her family in
the mountains with the Smith party.

the plight of Smith's slaves. Robert Owens was a black businessman and a very well respected citizen of Los Angeles. Biddy also had confided to Elizabeth Rowan, another well-known and respected black citizen of San Bernadino. Working together, Owens and Rowan were able to get the sheriffs of both Los Angeles and San Bernadino counties to stop Smith from taking his slaves out of the state.

The sheriffs, Robert Owens and ten of his vaqueros (cowboys) found the Smith party in the mountains. The sheriffs placed all the slaves in protective custody. Biddy served Smith with legal papers. She and the rest of the slaves would appeal to the court for their freedom.

Biddy and her group appeared before Judge Benjamin Hayes in Santa Monica, California. On the first day of the trial, Smith told the judge that these fourteen people were not his slaves but his hired help. Instead of paying them wages, he provided them with food and shelter.

He considered them a part of his family. They were moving to Texas with him willingly.

Biddy was unable to testify against Smith in the courtroom because of the Civil Practice Act of 1850, which stated that black people could not testify against white people in a court of law. Judge Hayes had to question Biddy and the other slaves in the chamber of his courtroom. Biddy told the judge and his two witnesses, "I have always done what I have been told to do; I always feared this trip to Texas, since I first heard of it. Mr. Smith told me I would be just as free in Texas as here." The other slaves stated, also, they did not know Texas was a slave state.

Judge Hayes was from the East coast and was opposed to slavery. He was certain that no slave would willingly move from a free state to a state which allowed slavery. He felt Smith took advantage of his slaves because they did not know how to read, write, or know their rights under the law.

Biddy was unable by law to testify
against Smith in a courtroom.

After listening to the testimony of Biddy and her group, Judge Hayes returned to the courtroom and told Smith he could not understand why Smith wanted to support an additional fourteen people. According to the court records, Smith owned only one suit and had five hundred dollars. He could barely afford to feed and support his wife and six children. Judge Hayes accused Smith of planning to sell his slaves once he got to Texas.

On January 21, 1856, Robert Smith failed to appear in court. Judge Hayes granted freedom to Biddy, her daughters, and the rest of Smith's slaves. He declared, "All men should be left to their own pursuit of freedom and happiness." Judge Hayes also said for the "petitioners to become settled and go to work for themselves— in peace and without fear."

Had this case been tried one year later, Biddy and her group probably would not have been granted their freedom. In 1857 the United

Judge Hayes grants freedom to Biddy, her
daughters, and the rest of Smith's slaves.

Biddy finds work to support herself and her daughters.

States Supreme Court ruled that slaves could not fight for their freedom in the courts. This was called the Dred Scott Decision. Slavery was not abolished in the United States until the end of the Civil War nine years later.

Now that Biddy was free, she needed to find work to support herself and her daughters. She did not have to look very far or wait very long for an opportunity to arise. During the trial she had caught the attention and admiration of one of the spectators. His name was Dr. John Strother Griffin, and he was the brother-in-law of Judge Hayes. Dr. Griffin had a medical practice in Los Angeles. He also was the official doctor for the Los Angeles County Jail and County Hospital. Dr. Griffin was impressed with Biddy's medical knowledge and the way she had represented herself and the others in court. He had need of a good midwife and nurse in his office. When he offered Biddy a job, she gratefully accepted his offer.

THE DRED SCOTT DECISION

Dred Scott was a slave who had been taken by his master from Missouri, a slave state, to Illinois, which was a free state and next to the Wisconsin territory. Slavery was not permitted in this region according to the Missouri Compromise (a measure taken by Congress to end the extension of slavery in national territory in 1821) which provided Maine to enter the Union as a free state and Missouri as a slave state. Abolitionists (people who were against slavery) helped Dred Scott sue for his freedom. On March 4, 1857, the Supreme Court ruled that the Missouri Compromise was unconstitutional: a slave did not become free when taken to a free state and was not entitled to the rights of a Federal citizen. It would take a civil war between the states of the north and south and the passing of the 14th Amendment to the Constitution in 1865 to give all blacks their freedom.

Next she accepted the invitation of Robert and Winnie Owens to live with them in Los Angeles until she found a rental unit. Around this time, Biddy, who did not have a last name, became known as Biddy Mason. No one is sure why she chose Mason for her last name.

Biddy began her work as a practical nurse for Dr. Griffin. Her big black bag became very familiar to families, both rich and poor of all ethnic groups. She became known as "Grandma Mason." After delivering a baby, Biddy sometimes was asked to stay a few days to cook, do laundry and care for the other children in the family while the new mother recovered. The women were happy to receive Biddy's special care. In addition to delivering babies and house-keeping, she also nursed sick prisoners in the County Jail and the County Hospital.

On October 16, 1856, Biddy's daughter Ellen married Charles Owens. Biddy was over-joyed. She knew the hard working and brave

Charles would be a good mate for her daughter.

Biddy always dreamed of owning a home. After ten years of hard work, she had saved enough money from her $2.50 per day salary to purchase property for a home. On November 28, 1866, she purchased ten acres of land on Spring Street for $250. This purchase made Biddy the first black woman to own land in Los Angeles. She was proud of her property and called it "the homestead." She saw it as a place to gather her family and friends, to help others, and plan community activities.

On the homestead, Biddy built rental units and leased space for businesses. In the back, near a spring, she grew her medicinal plants and herbs. On the advice of Dr. Griffin and Robert Owens, she bought and sold various parcels of land nearby. The profits from these sales made Biddy very wealthy.

In 1872, Biddy and a group of people founded the First African Methodist Episcopal

Biddy always dreamed of owning a house.

Church during one of the community meetings held in her home. This was the first black church in Los Angeles. Biddy paid all expenses and the taxes for the church property.

PROTEST

Although Biddy Mason was the founder of the First African Methodist Episcopal Church, she continued to attend the Fort Street Methodist Church, which had been established for whites. Apparently California law began to segregate churches and blacks could only attend churches founded by blacks. Some saw Biddy's attendance at the Fort Street Methodist Church as a political protest.

Biddy was also a member of a group who worked to provide schools for black children in Los Angeles. By law, black children were not allowed to attend public schools with white children. It was also illegal to establish separate

Biddy founded the first black church in Los Angeles.

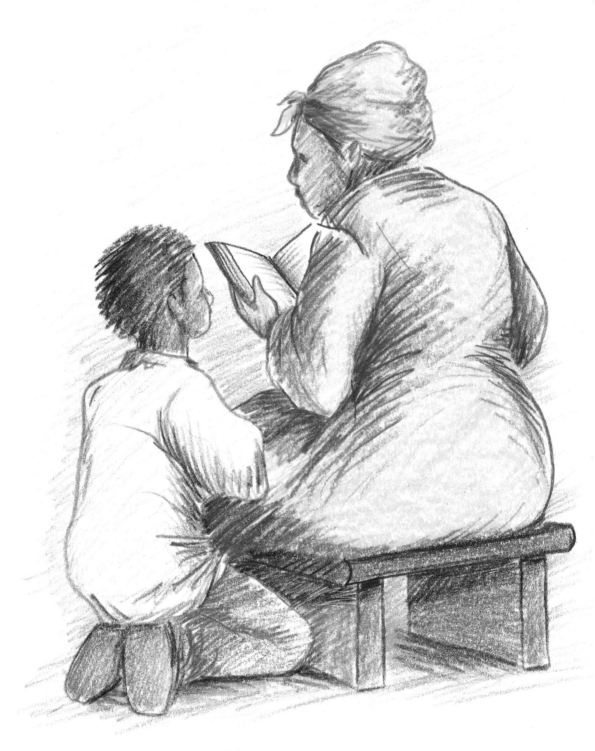

Biddy always helped children.

schools to educate them. Black families in Los Angeles who could afford to send their children away to school chose Oakland, California. Biddy's grandsons, Robert Curry Owens and Henry L. Owens were sent to Oakland to receive an education when they became school age. Biddy contributed a huge sum of money to fight this unfair law. Eventually, the law changed and separate school buildings were built in Los Angeles for black children.

Biddy's generosity was endless. She visited the prisoners in the County Jail daily. During the small pox epidemic in the 1860's she risked her

ELLEN MASON

Ellen Mason, Biddy's oldest daughter,
volunteered to teach
in the Sea Islands of South Carolina
in the fall of 1863.

own life to nurse others. She bought groceries and supplies for the families who became homeless during the floods. Biddy never turned away any needy person who stood on her porch, seeking her help. She was admired by many for her good deeds and heroic efforts.

By the mid 1880's, Biddy had witnessed the change in Los Angeles. Once a dusty cow town with a population of 1,600, Los Angeles had become a prosperous commercial city of 50,000 residents. She observed how the immigrants who were only skilled in agriculture struggled, earned low wages, and were unable to raise themselves from poverty. Biddy wanted her children and grandchildren to be able to support themselves and prosper.

Biddy and her daughter Ann opened and operated fourteen nursing homes in Los Angeles and San Bernadino. They cared for those who were ill or confined to a wheelchair and needed round the clock care. In 1885, Biddy deeded a

BROADWAY SPRING CENTER

The 333 South Spring Street property in Los Angeles that Biddy purchased for $250.00 in 1866 is now a $24 million dollar high rise shopping center and parking garage called the Broadway Spring Center.

part of her property to her grandsons so they could establish a livery stable. Robert ran this business with his brother Henry. Robert also had successful careers in politics and real estate.

In her later years, Biddy continued to receive visits from people seeking medical help, money and advice. She never turned anyone away. There was a long line of people waiting to see her on the morning of January 15, 1891, when Biddy died at the age of 73. The city mourned. In her obituary, the Los Angeles Times described Biddy as "a pioneer humanitarian who dedicated herself to forty years of good works." She was buried in a modest grave at Evergreen Cemetery in Boyle Heights.

Biddy Mason should be remembered as a courageous, intelligent, and generous woman who never forgot her humble beginnings. Her open hands gave freely of her services and wealth to those less fortunate than she.

On Palm Sunday, March 27, 1988, Mayor Tom Bradley and 3,000 appreciative citizens paid their respects to Biddy Mason. A large tombstone, which was donated by the congregation of the First African Methodist Episcopal Church, was unveiled at her grave.

November 16, 1989, was declared Biddy Mason Day. There was a special ceremony for the opening of a memorial to her in the Broadway Spring Center in downtown Los Angeles. The memorial celebrates the life of Biddy Mason. The dedication was attended by Biddy's great-granddaughter, Gladys Owens Smith. She recalled a family saying that Biddy had taught her children, and it was passed down to each generation: "If you hold your hand closed, Gladys, nothing good can come in. The open hand is blessed, for it gives in abundance, even as it receives."

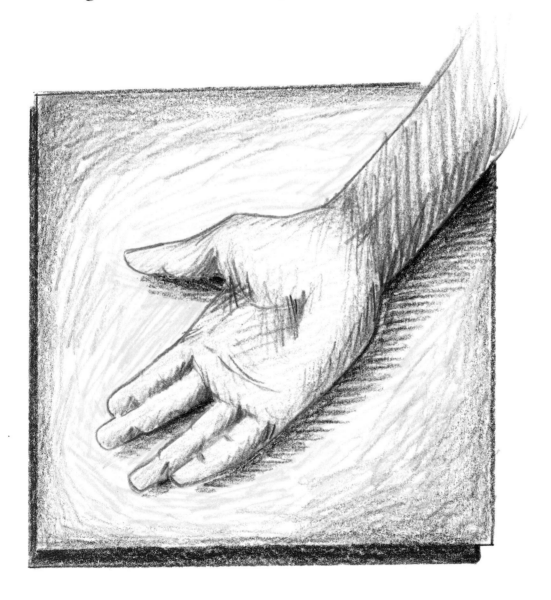

Biddy Mason 1818 – 1891

First AME

First African Methodist Episcopal Church
(First AME)
is the oldest black congregation, now
numbering 14,000 members,
in the city of Los Angeles.
Their motto is: "First to Serve."

Their mission is to improve the
economic conditions of communities through
job creation, career advancement,
business development, transportation, and
environmental awareness.

Some of their accomplishments are:
- Housing approximately 300 homeless
  persons during the winter
- Developing a bone marrow donor
  program
- Offering free tutoring, legal aid and
  computer training
- Establishing the Cecil L. Murray Education
  Center, which is an elementary school
  for children in grades K - 8

INDEX

About the Author

Deidre Robinson first learned about Biddy Mason while teaching California history to her fourth grade students at St. John Chrysostom School in Inglewood, California. She received her Bachelor of Arts degree in English from Pepperdine University and her Master of Arts degree in Education/Remedial Reading from Loyola Marymount University.

In 1996 Deidre was recognized in the fourth edition of *Who's Who Among America's Teachers*.

About the Artist

Albert T. Cooper, III received his Bachelor of Arts degree in Art from Xavier University. His most recent series of artwork expresses the importance, strength, and unity of the Family in our society. A native of Los Angeles, California, Albert currently lives in New Orleans, Louisiana.